THE LI
GROW

WILLIAM FORTT

THE LITTLE BOOK OF GROW-YOUR-OWN TIPS

WILLIAM FORTT

A.
Absolute Press

First published in Great Britain in 2011 by
Absolute Press
Scarborough House, 29 James Street West
Bath BA1 2BT, England
Phone 44 (0) 1225 316013 **Fax** 44 (0) 1225 445836
E-mail info@absolutepress.co.uk
Web www.absolutepress.co.uk

A catalogue record of this book is available from the British Library

ISBN 13: 9781906650667

Printed and bound in Malta on behalf of Latitude Press

‘I am better off with vegetables at the bottom of my garden than with all the fairies of *A Midsummer Night’s Dream*.’

Dorothy L. Sayers (1893–1957), English crime novelist

1

Grow as much as you can.

Even a tiny garden can produce something edible, and there are always sunny window sills and other places where plants in pots can grow happily. Make use of every space. Producing your own vegetables will give you immense satisfaction.

2

What soil have you got?

You could ask your neighbours, or just look for yourself. Pick some up, run it through your fingers and find out what it's made of. Is it heavy and sticky (clay), pale and stony (chalk), thin and dusty (sand), or dark and friable (silt)? Once you've identified the type, you can take action to improve it.

3

Clay soil needs the most work.

First, break it up: hack up the surface in autumn and leave the clods to be split by frost and rain. Then add plenty of humus (organic material), such as compost, seaweed, leafmould, dried grass mowings or animal manure. This will lighten and 'unstick' the clay and help water to drain away.

4

Light, sandy soils are the opposite of clay.

The wind blows them about, the rain soaks straight through, and they contain little goodness. Once again, the answer lies in the humus. Dig in large amounts of organic matter, which will improve the structure, making it heavier, more fertile and better at holding water.

5

Is your soil acid or alkaline?

You can buy a soil-testing kit, or use your common sense. Clay or peaty soils are acid, and need lime to help make them become more fertile. Soil above limestone or chalk is alkaline. This sort of ground suits most vegetables, and should not need any special treatment.

6

Get to know your vegetables.

There are, broadly speaking, four main groups: 1) potatoes, 2) roots (carrots, turnips, etc), 3) brassicas (cabbages, sprouts, etc), and 4) everything else (including onions, lettuce, beans and peas). Each group has different requirements, frailties and strengths.

7

Vegetable groups need to be rotated.

If you plant potatoes or brassicas in the same place every year, diseases and pests will build up in the soil. So divide the vegetable garden into four plots and rotate what you grow in each – spuds one year, roots the next, onions and salads the next, and so on.

8

Buy the best tools you can afford. A fork and a spade in stainless steel will last a lifetime and make digging easier. Other essentials are a rake, a hoe and a line with stakes at each end to mark out rows. A watering can and a good pair of gardening gloves will help, too.

9

Be selective.

If you have a massive garden, you can grow anything and everything you like. But if your space is limited, choose carefully. What do you like to eat most of? What grows best on your plot? What's most expensive to buy? What vegetables can you never find in the shops?

10

Start a compost heap.

Make a slatted wooden bin, or simply pile the compost up. Include vegetable waste from garden and kitchen (no citrus though), dried grass mowings, non-perennial weeds, torn card and newspaper, plus a sprinkling of earth. Turn the whole thing once and leave for at least three months.

11

Compost refuses to break down?

One problem may be lack of nitrogen. You can buy compost stimulants or ‘makers’ in the shops, but why not make use of a completely free liquid of which there is no shortage – human urine? Collect it in a bucket, dilute with water and pour over the heap.

12

Keep putting nutrients into the soil. Compost is good, but only goes so far. Your soil needs the correct balance of chemicals and trace elements. It can get these from blood, fish and bone meal, dried seaweed, animal manure and, best of all, volcanic rock dust (google it to find a supplier).

13

Get rid of weeds: method 1.

Pull them out by hand (making sure you extricate all the roots of perennial weeds). This is hard work which can only be done properly on your knees. But it is also effective, costs nothing and prevents accidental disturbance to growing vegetable plants. Do it little and often.

14

Use deep beds.

As the name suggests, deep beds are deeply dug. They are also no more than 1.2m (4ft) wide. This means you can reach the centre from either side without having to tread on the dug soil. As a result, the soil never gets compacted, and remains easy to weed and fork through.

15

Dig up rough ground with a spade rather than a fork.

You can dig up a clod, then chop it to pieces with the spade edge. Also use the spade to slice off the turfy top section and bury this upside down at the bottom of the trench, where it will rot down.

16

Get rid of weeds: method 2.

Hoe them. This cuts off roots just below the surface and leaves the tops to die. Advantages: it's speedy, and you can hoe standing up. Disadvantages: it leaves roots of perennials free to shoot again, and one false move can decapitate a vegetable seedling.

17

Save money on seeds.

Vegetable seeds can add up to quite a bill, so economise if you can. Buy the smallest packets available (you always need fewer than you think). Or form a cooperative with friends or neighbours, buy what you all need and then share them without wastage.

18

Bunyard's Exhibition or Hangdown Green (they're broad beans)?

Do your homework on vegetable varieties.

The choice is mind-numbing (several hundred varieties of tomato alone), but stay calm. Read up about the possibilities and pick whatever suits your needs. You can always try something different next year.

19

Get rid of weeds: method 3.

Blanket them in mulch. This deprives them of light and kills them. A mulch can be organic (grass clippings, compost, shredded bark, straw, manure, torn newspaper), which breaks down and improves the soil. Or unromantically inorganic (black polythene or old carpet), which doesn't.

20

Before sowing seeds, rake over the bed to obtain a fine tilth. Remove stones and other clutter. A fine and level tilth makes sowing and weeding easier, and gives the vegetables a more luxurious start in life. It also helps water to penetrate more evenly to the soil below.

21

Space rows and plants at the correct distance and depth. This is worth being fussy about, as spacing has a major effect on plant growth, and vegetables have different requirements. Follow the instructions on the seed packet, or consult a trustworthy guide such as *Charles Dowding's Organic Gardening* (Green Books).

22

Make your own measuring stick for seed sowing. Take a thin piece of batten, 1 metre long. Using paint or a felt-tip pen, plus a tape measure, mark out metric measurements on one side (in tens of centimetres). Then turn it over and do the same for imperial measurements (in 3-inch gradations).

23

Once you've measured out your rows, mark the ends with sticks.

Now use a small hoe to scrape out furrows between the sticks. If necessary, lay down a board to give you a straight edge. With practice, you'll be able to scrape straight lines freehand.

24

Water the furrows well before sowing.

This gets moisture under the seeds, ready to create a nice humid atmosphere to start them germinating. Use a can with a fine rose so that you don't swamp the soil and it stays fine and undisturbed.

25

Sow seeds sparingly.

Most of them will probably germinate, so avoid a tangled mat of seedlings coming up. This wastes seeds, and means you'll have to thin out and chuck away a lot of baby plants. Leave space between each seed. This takes longer and is fiddly, but will give you stronger plants.

26

Some **vegetables with a long growing life need wide spacing.** Luckily, these are often ones with big seeds, such as Swiss chard or parsnips, so they are easier to handle. Place groups of 3 seeds at 10cm (4in) intervals. You should get three seedlings at each spot, which you can easily thin down to one.

27

Once the seeds are in, draw back the soil with the rake to cover the furrows.

Take care not to disturb the seeds with vigorous raking. Tamp down the soil with the head of the rake. Mark the row, either with the crop's name written on a stick, or by stuffing the seed packet into a split piece of bamboo.

28

As carrots, turnips, spring onions and lettuce appear,

carefully thin the rows. This gives the remaining plants room to grow and stops them getting knotted up with their neighbours. It also gives you sweet and delicious baby vegetables to eat in salads.

29

Pick lettuce and other salad leaves singly

instead of hoiking up the entire plant. This avoids gaps in the row, and allows the plants to grow new leaves. Pick a few at a time from the outside of the lettuce. Do this regularly, and you should have a dependable supply of tender salads.

30

If you have room, grow the glorious globe artichoke

(it takes up a lot of space, but looks quite at home in a flower border). The best start is to obtain suckers from the base of an existing plant – ask a friend or neighbour. Artichokes planted in this way tend to last better than those grown from seed.

31

Sow broad beans in a block. They can grow tall, and are vulnerable to damage from high winds. If you have a nice solid rectangle of them, you can easily give them support by driving in stakes at the four corners, then stretching two or three lengths of twine tightly round them.

32

Save money on runner bean supports.

Instead of buying bamboo canes, find a handy source of hazel – a roadside hedge or a copse. Hazel grows fairly straight and thin for up to 2m (6ft), and will add a pleasingly bucolic touch to the veg patch. And it's free. But ask the landowner before you go cutting.

33

In hot summers, **climbing French beans can be amazingly prolific.** Leave a good proportion on the vines and let them dry out in the sun. By late autumn you'll be able to pull off the husky pods and harvest a crop of tasty dried beans to store for the winter. *Barlotto di Fuoco* is an excellent variety for drying.

34

Create a seed bed in a spare corner of the garden.

Here you can sow seeds of brassica, leek and other long-developing winter plants, without taking up space in the main beds. By summer, early potato and bean crops will be gone. Just the right time to transplant stuff from the seed bed into the newly-vacated soil.

35

It's tempting to grow too many courgette plants. Two are plenty for most households. Put 2 or 3 seeds in two stations 1 metre (3 foot) apart. When the seedling appears, protect it from predatory slugs by covering with the cut-off top from a plastic lemonade bottle.

36

Try growing scorzonera.

It's a strange and exotic root vegetable rarely seen in the shops. Long and thin, it grows easily and dives deep. Once you've peeled the black knobbly skin and gently steamed it, you have a white vegetable with an enigmatic hint of artichoke and asparagus.

37

Turnips are a doddle to grow and tasty to eat.

But they are at their very best when eaten young and small. This also allows you to make good use of the peppery foliage. Chop it and blanch it like spinach or chard. The same goes for young beetroot leaves.

38

Earth up your potatoes at least once,

and preferably twice after the leaves appear. Pull a ridge of soil carefully round the foliage with a draw hoe. This not only gets rid of weeds, but also encourages the plants to produce more tubers.

39

Brussels sprout plants grow tall and heavy,

especially if they develop a bumper crop. All this can be ruined by winds which rock the stems and weaken the roots. Give them support by driving in a stake by each plant and tying the two together with twine.

40

Protect your brassicas.

Cabbage white caterpillars (from eggs laid by butterflies) will munch them to death unless you take stern action. Spray the plants with soapy water or pick the creatures off by hand. In emergency cases, spray the leaves (carefully) with derris dust.

41

Onions will tend to 'bolt'

– get ready to flower – in hot dry weather. This will turn the plant into a thick and almost inedible stem with a small bulb. Stop the bolting process early on by pinching out the small flower stems which appear at the top of the plant – and by giving the bed a good soak.

42

Be generous with water.

In dry periods, you obviously need to irrigate your seeds and growing plants. The most effective way is to water gently and copiously every other day, thoroughly soaking the soil to as great a depth as possible. This is much better than simply wetting the surface every day.

43

Dig up your onions as soon as the foliage dies down.

Leave them too long and they may start to rot in damp weather. Just lift them gently out of the soil and let them dry out for a day or two. Better still, improvise a simple rack with wire mesh and spread the onions here.

44

Stringing onions is easy and impresses your friends.

Take a piece of twine 1 metre (3 foot) long, tie the ends together and hang from a suitable hook. Take an onion, insert the stalk at the bottom of the twine loop and weave it round. Take another and weave that in – and so on. It gets easier as the onion string gets heavier.

45

Lift main crop potatoes before the first frost

(probably in early October). Choose dry weather and dig them up in the morning. Leave on the surface to dry out through the day. Preferably turn them over so they dry on both sides.

46

Store potatoes in paper sacks

(your local greengrocer is a good source) or cardboard boxes. These allow the vegetables to breathe – plastic bags don't, causing a build-up of moisture and thus mould. Pick carefully through the potatoes as you store them. Keep only undamaged ones. Use others immediately.

47

Grow French marigolds (*tagetes*) next to brassicas.

The scent of the marigolds will draw cabbage white butterflies away from the cabbages to lay their eggs. This will save the vegetables from the depredations of the resulting caterpillars. Marigolds are also said to deter eelworms from attacking potatoes.

48

Garlic is one of the few veg you can plant in late autumn.

It needs a period of intense cold to develop properly. Push in single cloves in mid-October to late November, and by next summer you'll have a healthy crop. Hardneck varieties are hardiest and give most bang for your buck (as they say).

49

Keep the garden as full as possible.

Bare soil generally means nothing growing, which is a waste. When one crop finishes, clean up and bung in another. And if you've planted something slow-growing (like potatoes), sow a fast-growing 'catch crop' such as radish or rocket on top, and harvest that first.

50

Plan to have a continuous supply of veg through the year. This takes careful thought and some ingenuity, but you should be able to pick fresh produce from January (sprouts, parsnips, kale) through the bounty of summer until Christmas (carrots, cabbage, oriental greens, leeks and many more).

William Fortt

William Fortt is a keen gardener and environmentalist who delights in minimalizing personal waste and enjoys finding and sharing ways to save and prolong our resources. He has been an author for more than 30 years, with many books to his name, including *The Little Book of Gardening Tips* and *The Little Book of Green Tips* (also Absolute Press).

THE LITTLE BOOK OF
BARBECUE
TIPS
ANDREW LANGLEY

THE LITTLE BOOK OF
BEER
TIPS
ANDREW LANGLEY
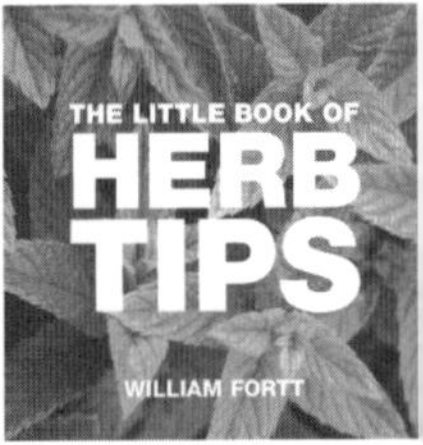
THE LITTLE BOOK OF
HERB
TIPS
WILLIAM FORTT
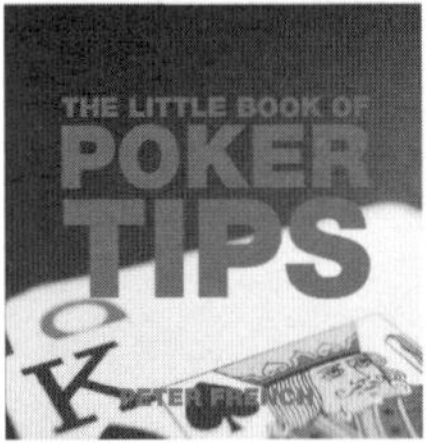
THE LITTLE BOOK OF
POKER
TIPS

THE LITTLE BOOK OF
GARDENING
TIPS
WILLIAM FORTT
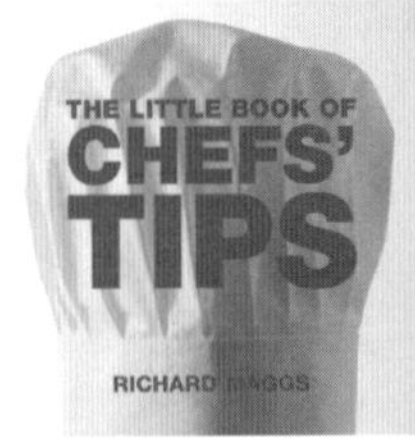
THE LITTLE BOOK OF
CHEFS'
TIPS
RICHARD

THE LITTLE BOOK OF
SPICE
TIPS
ANDREW LANGLEY

THE LITTLE BOOK OF
GOLF
TIPS
PETER FRENCH

THE LITTLE BOOK OF
TIPS
SERIES

THE LITTLE BOOK OF
CHEESE
TIPS
ANDREW LANGLEY

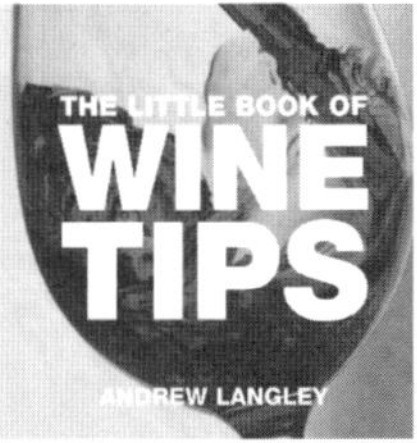
THE LITTLE BOOK OF
WINE
TIPS
ANDREW LANGLEY

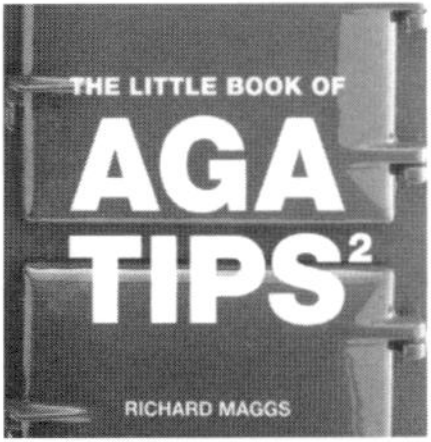
THE LITTLE BOOK OF
AGA
TIPS 2
RICHARD MAGGS

THE LITTLE BOOK OF
COFFEE
TIPS
ANDREW LANGLEY

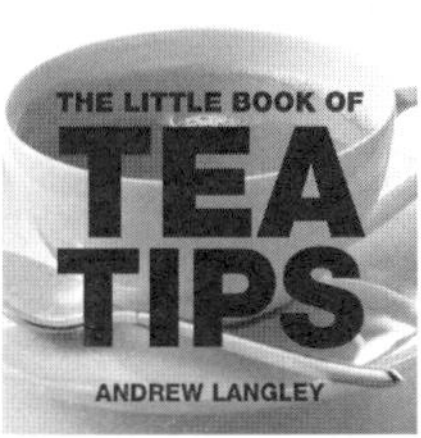
THE LITTLE BOOK OF
TEA
TIPS
ANDREW LANGLEY

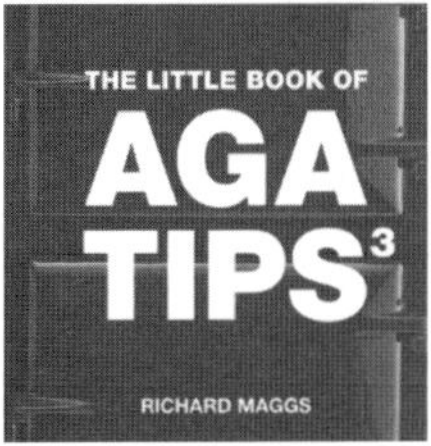
THE LITTLE BOOK OF
AGA
TIPS 3
RICHARD MAGGS

THE LITTLE BOOK OF
AGA
TIPS
RICHARD MAGGS

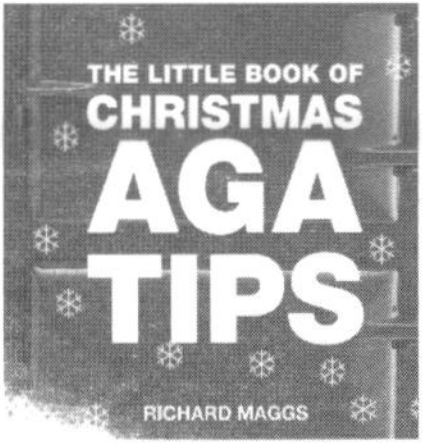
THE LITTLE BOOK OF
CHRISTMAS
AGA
TIPS
RICHARD MAGGS

THE LITTLE BOOK OF
RAYBURN
TIPS
RICHARD MAGGS

THE LITTLE BOOK OF
BRIDGE
TIPS
PETER FRENCH

THE LITTLE BOOK OF
CHESS
TIPS
PETER FRENCH

THE LITTLE BOOK OF
FISHING
TIPS
MICK DEVENISH

THE LITTLE BOOK OF
GREEN
TIPS
WILLIAM FORTT

THE LITTLE BOOK OF
KITTEN
TIPS
ANDREW LANGLEY

MARMITE
PAUL HARTLEY
THE LITTLE BOOK OF
MARMITE
TIPS

THE LITTLE BOOK OF
PUPPY
TIPS
ANDREW LANGLEY

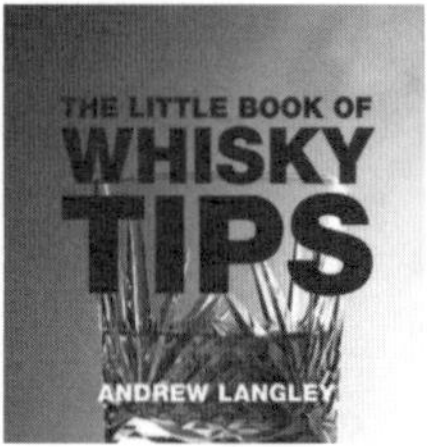
THE LITTLE BOOK OF
WHISKY
TIPS
ANDREW LANGLEY

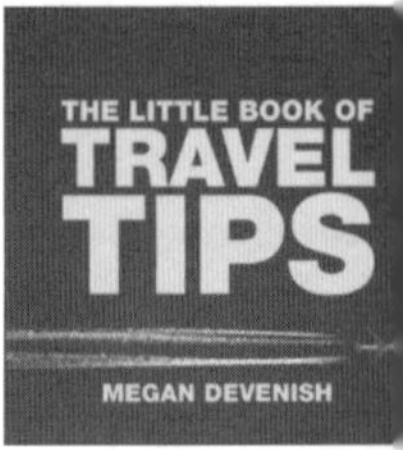
THE LITTLE BOOK OF
TRAVEL
TIPS
MEGAN DEVENISH

Little Books of Tips from Absolute Press

Aga Tips
Aga Tips 2
Aga Tips 3
Backgammon Tips
Barbecue Tips
Beer Tips
Bread Tips
Bridge Tips
Cake Decorating Tips
Cheese Tips
Chefs' Tips
Chess Tips
Chocolate Tips
Christmas Aga Tips
Chutney and Pickle Tips
Cocktail Tips
Coffee Tips
Curry Tips
Fishing Tips
Frugal Tips
Gardening Tips
Golf Tips
Green Tips
Grow Your Own Tips
Herb Tips
Houseplant Tips
Jam Tips
Kitten Tips
Macaroon Tips
Marmite Tips
Olive Oil Tips
Pasta Tips
Poker Tips
Puppy Tips
Rayburn Tips
Spice Tips
Tea Tips
Travel Tips
Whisky Tips
Wine Tips
Vinegar Tips